MONEY GAME
WINNER

How to win one of life's most exciting contests

Ben Carlsen

PALM
SPRINGS
PUBLISHING

PSP

BEN CARLSEN

MONEY GAME WINNER

Copyright © 2012   **by Dr. Ben A. Carlsen, MBA**

www.moneygamewinner.com

ISBN: 978-1-62050-391-1
Library of Congress Control no: 2012937544
www.moneygamewinner.com

Published by: Palm Springs Publishing
2012
Los Angeles, Ca., Miami, Fl., New York, NY.
www.palmspringspublishing.com
Printed in USA

Disclaimer: This book is for educational purposes only. Recommendations regarding the self-help strategies herein are based on the author's experience, knowledge and research. The publisher, and/or the author assume no liability for any financial losses or obligations which may be incurred by following the advice, recommendations, or suggestions offered.

Financial actions entail risk, and poor choices may result in adverse consequences. Readers are advised to seek expert advice from Attorneys, CPA's, Financial Planners, Tax law experts, Real Estate brokers or other appropriate professionals before taking risks and/or making significant financial decisions.

From the Author of:

Bites of Business
Personal Financial Survival
25 Mistakes that can Prevent You from
Financial Success
Confessions of an Overspender

"You have to learn the rules of the game. And then you have to play better than anyone else.

Albert Einstein

Preface

Get ready for an adventure. An exciting look at an exciting game. A game we all play. Where the quality of our play can determine the quality of our life. The Money Game.

There are numerous books on personal finance. Generally those books focus on savings and investments. They offer good, solid advice about how to make your money grow and how to create a budget and live within it. They provide information about taxes, real estate, retirement plans, stocks and bonds. I highly recommend that you read some of these books and believe that they will help you in your quest for financial success.

I've written those more traditional "money books" including: *Personal Financial Survival.* This time I wanted to take a new approach because I'm convinced that lots of folks have extensive financial and investment knowledge and still don't do well. I also know that many more haven't the foggiest notion of where to begin. Most readers probably fall somewhere between those extremes.

I realized that financial success has more to do with other factors. You could read a hundred books on personal finance and still not be able to effectively manage your finances because you have the wrong mindset, attitude, or skill-set. I chose to look at it from a game perspective realizing that some players consistently win at games while others regularly lose. What if personal finance is a game? A game you can win.

When I completed an early draft of *Money Game Winner* I was surprised and pleased with the considerable positive feedback from readers and friends. Several of those readers wanted more specifics and supporting details. So I decided to include some of those elements along with steps and formulas designed to help operationalize the philosophy and concepts. I'm sure these changes strengthened the book. This may be a skinny book but it packs a major punch!

As with most challenges in life whether it's love, money, personal satisfaction, spirituality, or physical health it all begins with that three pound mass of neural tissue housed in our head. In the following pages you will use that organ to explore a novel way of looking at money and financial progress. You will learn new strategies for success and re-inforce constructive habits and techniques. The objective being to help you become a stronger competitor and be better prepared to win the Money Game.

ACKNOWLEDGEMENTS

Special thanks to all who helped and/or stood by me in creating this book, and in particular:

Roberto Montanez (formatting & editing), Greg Borowski (cover design), Elsie Delva-Smith (inspiration), Krzysztof Bryniuk (support), and Hendrick Ferguson (proofing & editing).

"Winning isn't the most important thing.
It's the only thing."

Vince Lombardi

CONTENTS

INTRODUCTION

You've played games all your life. You probably considered games and "real life" as distinctly separate. We want to challenge that notion.

This book is for everyone having trouble paying their bills, dissatisfied with their financial progress; aiming for financial success or wealth or those who have already attained it. You should read this book if you see yourself as a Winner or if you want to change your "luck." In fact, everyone can benefit from the concepts, principles, strategies, plans and tips presented here. As a teacher I believe that it is perhaps most valuable for young adults and twenty-something's who are trying to figure out their life's ambitions, career choices and place in the economic world. I know it took me many years and lots of mistakes. Whatever your age and financial status in these pages you will discover a new way of thinking about money and a philosophy of life that embraces personal financial success as a way of acting and living.

Life can be viewed as a game. The game of life is a high stakes pursuit in which some are more successful than others; it has a beginning and an end, and new players will emerge and compete. Likewise with the Money Game. Everyone who plays the game of life will also be a player of the Money Game.

In this book you will learn about the game, its importance to you and some strategies for successful competition. As a result you may also question or revise your perspectives about money, success, fairness, and your values and ambitions.

As in every game there are rules, winners and losers, strategies and luck involved. The game is complex and of lengthy duration. In fact, it lasts a lifetime. Some begin the game with an advantage. Many start with handicaps or play in a game of smaller stakes, more desperate competitors, or one that is "rigged" in some way to disadvantage certain players.

The goal of the Money Game is to compete successfully so that your winnings are sufficient to meet the objectives that you have set for yourself. Some players are satisfied with modest winnings while others are driven to win hugely. Some are vicious players who will violate, ignore or change the rules to suit themselves. In some cases there are penalties for even minor infractions, while some players may be able to get away with profuse cheating.

Stockbrokers and money managers have long considered the equities market to be a game. This mentality served them well, but sometimes at the expense of individual investors, the general business community and the society at large. Nobel Prize-winning economist Adam Smith wrote about this concept almost a half-century ago. However, the game is not, and has never been, limited to the stock market. The Money Game is broad and pervasive encompassing all of business and commerce, as well as government rule-makers, investors, and facilitators. The sub-games of stocks, bonds, commodities, banking, real-estate, manufacturing, education, healthcare, retail, professional services, public service, transportation, information technology, and so on are components of the vast overall game. They can be thought of as "games within the game." And some games have better reputations and outcomes than others, and some players within those games do too.

The Money Game can be exciting, frightening, tedious, fun, rewarding, challenging, frustrating, and entails many other emotions. The rewards for winning can be substantial for an individual player, a family, future generations, a community or a nation. Since everyone plays the game everyone knows something about it. Certain people seem to have a natural affinity for the game and appear to win without much effort while others struggle for years and can never seem to get ahead.

Americans love games and competition, but often they are content with being spectators. However, you can't afford to remain on the sidelines in the Money Game. So get yourself psyched up so that you can be an effective participant, a forceful competitor, and ultimately a WINNER of the MONEY GAME.

"Games lubricate the body and the mind."

Benjamin Franklin

CHAPTER ONE

Understanding the Game

In this book I make the case for viewing your personal finances as a game. A really important and challenging one and one that is more pervasive in this society than perhaps any other on the planet. You may think, why play? The answer is simple – you have to! And why play well, or hard? Because there are major incentives to play well and substantial benefits for winning. Let's explore this concept a little further.

The Case for Winning

As with any concept as powerful as this one it is characterized by numerous myths, folklore, "old wives tales," common sense approaches, success and horror stories. Let's examine and perhaps debunk, or at least call into question a few of these.

Does MONEY lead to POWER? –
Money and power go hand in hand. No question about it. Whenever someone has a disproportionate share of a highly valued commodity (money) they have de facto power. And they can choose to exercise that power, share it or give it away.

Does MONEY equate with SUCCESS? –
There are people who are successful but remain poor, or at least don't amass real wealth. Consider Mother Teresa, Martin Luther King Jr, Gandhi, Albert Einstein, and various political, academic or religious leaders. However, the most common contemporary measure of success is financial.

Does MONEY give you FREEDOM? –
The poor in many parts of the world are oppressed, disen-
franchised, unable to relocate or exercise any meaningful
measure of self-determination. Money provides you with
freedom of choice. Not merely whether to eat at *McDonald's* or *Burger King*, but to eat Sushi or Prime Rib or dine
in the South of France. It will allow you to travel, explore
your desires and expand your options for indulgence or ful-
fillment.

Does making MONEY require INTELLIGENCE? --
We know that the relationship between money and intelligence is tenuous at best. Are the smartest people the
richest? Obviously not! Aside from having a basic level of
intelligence other factors will play a larger role.

Is a college EDUCATION necessary to make MONEY? --
Not at all. But it can help you prepare for a high paying career. Of course there are plenty of examples of college or
even high school dropouts becoming extraordinarily successful. Some are millionaires or even became billionaires
(like Bill Gates and Steve Jobs).

Do you have to be LUCKY to make MONEY? –
I'm sure you've heard the saying "I'd rather be lucky than
smart!" And with money that may be true.

Although intelligence will help-- luck, good fortune and
good timing will often make the difference in winning or
losing the Money Game and by what margin. Can you improve your luck? Some people would say yes.
Some applicable lore is: "Luck is when preparation meets
opportunity," and "The harder I work the luckier I get."

Does it require hard WORK to win at the MONEY GAME?--

Not necessarily. If it did the hardest workers would be the richest. Do you see the laborers, trash collectors, coal miners, and clerks retiring early with vast wealth? Often the hardest working people are the most poorly compensated.

Does MONEY lead to HAPPINESS? –

Various surveys have reported that residents of countries with higher GNP are not necessarily happier. And it appears that culture and climate may have something to do with it.

People who have means but live in depressing societies or locales are at least able to escape and find happiness elsewhere either temporarily or permanently. You can be miserable whether you're rich or poor.

Can MONEY make it easier to find LOVE? –

They say "money can't buy love," and that's probably true. But neither can poverty!

Rules of the Game

The rules of the Money Game are quite complex, convoluted, with many exceptions and not uniformly enforced. There can be many winners simultaneously and consecutively. The rules do not specify what constitutes winning. Likewise they do not define losing. These terms are not explained and are left to the individual and collective players' perceptions.

Although the rules are flexible and ever-changing it helps immensely to have a basic understanding at a given point in time. And since everyone's a player they want their piece of the "action."

The government wants a share, businesses do too, as well as merchants and practically everyone you encounter.

Rule changes can be disruptive or change your odds. For example, let's say the government decides to change the income tax rules, or the banks decide to change their loan requirements, or *FICO* changes the way they calculate credit scores. As you can appreciate any or all of these rule changes could be game changers. And so many entities have access and ability to modify the rules it's a full time job just to try and keep track of the rule changes. This is where you might require expert advice.

Recently there has been substantial turmoil in the general economy which has greatly impacted strategies, success factors, competition and results. The recession that began in 2008 has been long, deep and painful. Those playing by the rules extant prior to that period may have been adversely impacted or wiped out. Particularly those employing the strategy of maximum leveraging for real estate purchases, assuming that real estate prices would always rise, and using equity loans for funding. Overall economic impacts have been major with business curtailments, people losing jobs, reduced bank lending, foreclosures, etc.

The rules are constantly in flux. What it takes to win at one point may not work at another. Situations can change rapidly so you must constantly "'sense" the environment, keep abreast of financial and equity market changes, and prepare to anticipate and strategically adapt to new conditions. Those who are informed and nimble can exploit opportunities and gain from volatility.

The length of the game is not specified and it is uncertain when any player will stop playing. The game ends when you do, although the others will go on playing. Participants enter and exit the contest constantly. And when you quit playing your accumulated winnings will be distributed to other players. Good players will anticipate this and try to retain as much of their earnings as possible to direct to their favorite surviving players.

"Money was never a big motivation for me,
except as a way to keep score.
The real excitement is playing the game."

Donald Trump

CHAPTER TWO

Preparation for the Game

In our society we don't do a good job of preparing players for the Money Game. Few public high schools have mandatory courses in Personal Finance and many high school graduates don't even know the basics. And it's getting worse. A recent (2012) study of "millennials," those arriving at adulthood around the turn of the 21st century, found that ignorance about simple financial concepts, terms and practices is pervasive. An article in *USA TODAY* Money (4/18/12) reported on the results of a study conducted by the *Jumpstart Coalition for Financial Literacy*. The results: high school seniors scored an average of 57.3% in 1997 and 48.3% in 2008. Less than half of the questions on the test answered correctly!! That's an "F" in any class.

Here's the scenario. The Money Game is getting tougher, the stakes are higher, the playing field more uncertain, the players less competent, and the competitors increasingly desperate.

If you have bad luck, bad timing and poor preparation are you doomed? Probably. But the Money Game is a long game and a very forgiving one. Unlike most games you play that last only an hour or two, in the years and decades you play the Money Game you will have many opportunities to prepare, and cycles of a favorable play environment. So hang in there and watch the character of the game as it unfolds. Get ready for your strategic and explosive moves and your game winning plays.

Financial Literacy

Illiterates can't read. Financial illiterates can read this book but can't read a financial statement or annual report. It is important to have a level of competence in understanding basic financial terminology and concepts. But as we see the "millennials" aren't as savvy as they should be, and the more mature players aren't either. In this game just a little more expertise can make you a standout.

"On the job" (or in the game) education is fine and just living in a society like ours gives you exposure to a lot of financial information. You will hear or see stock market reports daily, even on your *Smartphone*. Your annual salary increase may be tied to the inflation rate. You know about consumer pricing through regular shopping excursions. Your employer will typically offer a range of benefits including a 401K plan. The government will regularly release statistics on the inflation rate, unemployment rate and consumer confidence levels. You know about credit card interest rates, cell phone carrier charges, cable fees and so forth. A few people take the extra steps to become even more knowledgeable, and a percentage of those do heavy research.

There are numerous sources to enhance your financial literacy both internet and printed, free and fee. Here are some examples of paid subscription publications: *Money, Smart Money, Consumer's Digest, AAII* (American Association of Individual Investors) *Journal*. And some others: *Wall Street Journal, Barron's, Bottom Line, Forbes, Fortune*.

And popular on-line and *Smartphone* resources like: *yahoofinance.com, bloomberg.com, fool.com, money.com, morningstar.com, investorguide.com, thestreet.com, etc.*

Or for cable TV watchers *CNBC, CNNMoney or Bloomberg Channel* are good choices.

In this era of internet education there are some excellent FREE sites to help you become financially literate: *CrashCourse.org* (a great site sponsored by the National Endowment for Financial Information); *BankRate.com* (debt related info.); *EducationCents.org* (Colorado Dept. of Higher Education); *Spendster.org* (a confessional site where people have reported over $4 billion in wasteful purchases); and *MyMoney.gov* (U.S. Financial literacy website). Happy Surfing!

There are also college courses, free sponsored seminars, employer educational sessions, paid courses, etc. As you can see there is no dearth of information out there. It all depends how deep you want to go.

More Important Preparation

I suspect that your most important preparation will result from your decision to become a better player and the mindset that will require. And information alone won't do it. We're all aware of the many financial experts and gurus who have got into difficulty.

Mental and motivational preparation is, I believe, the biggest edge you can have in the Money Game. You can, and will, learn specifics along the way; you will also learn from your mistakes and successes and from those of others. However, even though this is a common path it is a rather inefficient way to proceed.

Your commitment to the Money Game will cause you to be more aware and open. You will seek expert advice as necessary. I'm sure you can find useful, inspirational and motivational ideas, resources, concepts, strategies and techniques on these pages. Your decision to purchase this book may be an important step in your Money Game preparation. Of course the discipline to read it and apply the ideas are essential.

CHAPTER THREE

Playing the Game

You're already a player. It's only a matter of learning more about the game and how to win it. To become a more informed and successful competitor.

As lottery players are fond of saying, "you can't win if you don't play!" They use this statement as justification for their gambling and you can't argue with the logic. And what's wrong with it? If you're spending a few bucks here and there and have hopes and dreams (fantasies may be a better term) of being a big winner, isn't that good thing? Many would argue yes.

In the Money Game of life you can limit your risk, improve your odds of winning, and make strategic decisions and plans that will in large measure assure your potential for success. You have far more control than you would in games of pure chance and that feature is enticing. But you need to know how to play.

Competition

Life is competitive. There are winners and losers. Some people are more competitive than others. Competitors are frequently vying for the same scarce resources, assets, careers, deals, jobs, etc. A competitive spirit, ambition, desire, determination, etc. are all valuable qualities in meeting and besting competitive challenges.

Your competitors in the Money Game are extensive.

There will be direct competitors like your co-workers, other job seekers, or someone making an offer on a house or business you want to buy, and indirect competitors like those involved in financing, or providing you with goods or services.

You may not be accustomed to viewing the merchant, your government, a neighbor, your banker, or your employer as your competitor and it may not meet a strict interpretation of the term. However, any institution, business, or person who is trying to gain more of your money or assets is in some sense a competitor. They're competing for your resources and you're competing for theirs. I'm not implying it's a "zero-sum" game where for every winner there's a proportionate loser, but I would argue that there are lots of folks competing with you and for control of your assets. And, of course, in a broader sense WE ARE ALL COMPETITORS IN THE MONEY GAME.

Games We Can Learn From

There are many games to choose from which employ strategies that are instructive for mastery of the Money Game. These games are popular and competitive and their potential applicability to your personal real-life Money Game will readily become apparent. We will now discuss a few of them.

Monopoly

In the classic board game *Monopoly* (Parker Bros./Hasbro), the player that concludes the game with the greatest combined accumulation of assets (cash and property) is declared the winner.

Players can win and lose money, buy and sell properties, railroads and utilities, charge other players rent or fees for the use of their assets, pay taxes, go bankrupt, become insolvent; even go to jail. The game has been popular since the Great Depression and is the best-selling board game of all time because in many ways it emulates the realities of the financial world.

Applicable strategies for the real-life Money Game in some measure parallel those of the board game. Players in the board game soon learn the value of purchasing properties, improving real estate by erecting homes and hotels on their land, increasing the value and charging correspondingly higher rents.

The player also learns that acquiring a monopoly of properties, utilities, or transportation companies gains increasing financial bounty, and that properties located in more affluent areas cost more, but reap more in value and revenue. There are also little peculiarities in the rules that favor the well-informed. For example, the monetary gains from rent jump disproportionately from two to three houses on a given property. Smart players who have two houses on one of their properties will recognize the rule irregularity and will quickly add another house to take advantage of this favorable condition.

Chess

The game of chess is a traditional game of competition and strategy with the objective to win the battle and capture the King of the opposing empire. It is a game of strategy and *control*.

To be effective contenders/players must learn the rules, know themselves, understand their opponent, know how the game pieces move (their advantages and limitations) and learn strategies.

Control of the center of the board is a basic principle. This is valuable because the player controlling the center has more options. Think about it. If your Knight is stuck in a corner how will he be able to exercise his substantial powers of mobility in attacking your opponent, capturing his pieces and gaining advantage? Whereas if he is closer to the center his potential range of impact is much greater, and his strategic utility for the King is enhanced.

Other game-winning principles include: protection of the King; early moves are important to the outcome; threatening moves are desirable; every piece can make a difference (even the lowly pawn); keep your most powerful force (the Queen) in reserve until late in the game, because she is such a valuable asset and such a potentially devastating loss.

In the real-life Money Game *strategy and control* are of utmost importance too. You need to plan your advance, anticipate moves by the competition, conserve your resources, and ultimately be aggressive in your drive to win.

War Games

In addition to *Monopoly* and *Chess* games and business corollaries, military theory and war games might help us in understanding how to win. It is difficult to imagine situations more compelling than armed conflict, battles and war. Let's look at some classic strategies.

Sun Tzu's, *Art of War* is a helpful resource. His strategies have been studied in Military Colleges, Business Schools, and by leaders of all ilk. Sun Tzu emphasizes plans based on rational analysis, knowledge, wisdom and understanding, and learning from past victories and defeats. He advises: be prepared, stay focused on your objectives, apply strategies and tactics to the situation at hand, protect your resources, and don't be controlled by your emotions. He stresses patience, positioning and adaptation.

The "divide and conquer" strategy is a winning one when confronted with a superior force. And, in life you would be smart not to take on all opponents or obstacles at once but to attack your challenges piecemeal, albeit strategically.

Perhaps his most intriguing advice has to do with deception. Sun Tzu's winning approaches employ deceptive techniques. There is value in deception. It misleads your opponent perhaps causing him to over- or under- estimate his adversary's strength, misinterpret your intent, employ ineffective counter-measures, make unnecessary concessions, etc. And it gives you the advantage of "surprise."

Sports

If you follow team sports you will also see some common denominators. Not only do the teams engage in extensive talent recruitment efforts finding and acquiring the best available players, and spend money, resources and time in the process, they devote lots of effort in training and developing their personnel.

The owners hire coaches and support staff, they conduct research into their competitors' game plans, strengths and weaknesses; they develop strategies to exploit the other team's weaknesses and neutralize their strengths. They develop into a cohesive team focused on the game.

With the best talent, the best "intelligence," the best preparation, the best game plan, and heightened motivation, they can be a competitive force to be reckoned with and have a good shot at winning. And so it is in life. And so it is in the Money Game.

Individual players generally have innate talent, but spend considerable time practicing play, developing their skills and learning how to aggressively and effectively play within the rules (and/or use the rules to advantage). They also learn to play together capitalizing on their combined strengths.

These same requirements will help your attain victory in your Money Game.

Video Games

Video games have surged in popularity over the past decade or so. They provide for individual or multi-player competition using computers, displays and sophisticated software, in a fast-paced environment with complex protocols, rules and scenarios. Most games are a type of complex, interactive "puzzle." Typically they require the player to process information rapidly and make decisions instantly. For a player to become proficient requires quick-thinking, good strategy, practice, dedication and knowledge, as well as superior eye-hand coordination.

There is a stratification of players, just as in the Money Game, starting out with the *Newbie* (new to the game) and *Noob* (a derogatory term for someone who will not or cannot learn); and moving up the hierarchy. At the top of the game there are some very SERIOUS players. *Expert Gamers* and *Uber Gamers*!

The information processing requirements, decision-making skills, competitive mind-set, strategic and tactical planning and related proficiencies are clearly transferable and beneficial in the Money Game.

Business

You don't have to think of yourself and your family using a Monopoly, Chess, War Games, Video Games or a sports analogy, but you'd better think in terms of business.

The business model is probably the most applicable and useful for you. Businesses are in business to make money. So are you! Businesses have competition. You also inhabit a competitive world. Businesses have cycles; ups and downs. So do you. Businesses develop success strategies and so must you. Businesses must contain costs and may find it necessary to reduce expenses. You will too! We will further explore this area later in the book. For now, just remember:
THINK OF YOURSELF AS A BUSINESS!

In business, as in the games we discussed, the objective is to keep moving forward. In fact the primary purposes of business are generally agreed to be "Growth and Profitability." That is, the business needs to grow, expand, move forward and be profitable in the process.

You've seen small "mom and pop" stores develop into larger, more profitable enterprises. Once the momentum is in place it is easier to maintain it. But if the business is shrinking instead of expanding there will be unpleasant consequences, as we will discuss later.

Similarly in your personal finances the business model requires that you advance. Your goal should be to have more assets next year than this one, and to consistently make more money along the way. Keep in mind that the results are not decided until the end of the game although there are many benchmarks along the way. As in any game a number of moves or plays will determine the score at the end of the first round, period, quarter, etc., and ultimately at game end.

Often players make intense efforts to establish dominance early in the game and again during the final minutes. In the Money Game this corresponds to roughly your twenties or thirties for the early effort and perhaps fifties (and even sixties) for that final push. For most players your game playing peaks before retirement. However, even if you retire you will continue playing in a different arena typically characterized by less intense, but more strategic and conservative play. At this stage of the game let the younger players "showboat" and encourage them along their way. If they're smart they will appreciate your support, wisdom and experience.

There is much to be learned from the games, approaches and strategies we discussed in this chapter, as well as from the manipulative, strategic, political or power plays presented by authors like Machiavelli in *The Prince,* or even Donald Trump (e.g. *The Art of the Deal).*

My intent is not to overwhelm you with theories, approaches, and game examples but to stimulate your thinking and appreciation for the complexity of the Money Game and the framework for developing a winning strategy.

"All men can see these tactics
whereby I conquer, but what none can see is the
strategy out of which victory evolved."

-Sun Tzu

CHAPTER FOUR

Strategies of the Game

Now let's personalize your strategy. Accumulation of wealth, taking chances, limiting risk, dealing with financial institutions, and of course, LUCK, are all elements of the game. It clearly demonstrates the competitive nature of the scenario and the players when it comes to any form of the Money Game.

Players in the real-life Money Game may not play for amusement, or perhaps not even the thrill of victory. They're often playing for survival, success, independence or peace of mind, although it can be FUN.

The Playing Field

The landscape of the Money Game is constantly changing. In the previous chapter the playing field was a "board," a "court," a computer screen, a playing field, business or profession or a battlefield. In real-life the playing field is broad, encompassing everything that's financial in your life, and it doesn't remain static. The changing nature of the landscape complicates the game and requires exceptional skill by a successful competitor. Whereas in primitive or third world countries changes may be gradual and evolutionary, in modern nations the change is revolutionary, year-to-year and day-by-day. So strategies and techniques that served you well some years back may not suffice or give you a competitive edge today.

Your selection of a field in which to work or practice, or continuing with our game analogy – to *play* - is extremely important.

With regard to income, the Money Game is structured to reward certain players more than others. High paying professions are well known, and so are the low ones. So depending on the value you place on earnings you will want to choose wisely and early. And don't be afraid to change if you're dissatisfied with the way the game is going for you. Career changes can happen at any stage and we're all familiar with "late bloomers" like Colonel Sanders (*KFC*) who used his Social Security retirement income to start his fried chicken empire.

To succeed you must recognize and adapt to changes in the financial and economic landscape and these can occur at any time. Changes to the landscape of the game will advantage some players and interfere with others' progress. For example if you chose to play as a "Knight" (soldier/warrior) some years back you wouldn't have been able to make a living. Current Knights at least are able to survive, earn decent compensation (comparatively) and have career advancement opportunities. Similarly professions like nursing, teaching, firefighters and policemen had meager salaries. The landscape for these professions has dramatically changed and many are now high earners, well above typical working class standards. You might do well to choose your profession wisely and play strategically and expertly within the rules and confines of that sub-set of the general Money Game.

Game Theory

Economists, mathematicians, psychologists, sociologists, philosophers, or other social scientists are all interested in game theory and specifically in trying to analyze, forecast and predict human behavior particularly in regard to rational economic decision-making.

In other words, why you make the decisions you do, and how can you improve these decisions.

The concept of *utility* is the most common denominator. Our economic decision-making is in large measure believed to be determined by the utility, usefulness, or value to us of the thing or service in question. The higher the perceived utility the more likely we are to value, pursue, and ultimately acquire it. We are trading our resources, effort, talent, money, work, for the object(s) of our desires. This appears to make sense and is therefore suspected to represent rationality. Of course it doesn't tell the whole story. Emotions, aesthetics and preferences always enter the realm of decision-making to one degree or another. And valence (as I learned as an undergrad) does too. Valence being our degree of attraction (or aversion) to the object in question. Moreover, morality can enter the decision process as some alternatives may be viewed as inconsistent with societal or personal beliefs.

Most of the game theory constructs involve mathematical analysis of decision options and related variables. The so-called *Nash Equilibrium* (remember Russell Crowe in *A Beautiful Mind*?) postulates that if everyone has the same information, the decisions will be rational, equal, and predictable. However, disturbances in the equilibrium will result from participants employing novel or deviant strategies, or from information imbalance.

One game is particularly interesting. It's called the "Prisoner's Dilemma" and entails a scenario where two individuals are arrested.

But the police have insufficient evidence to convict either one of them without convincing one or both to betray the other by "ratting," "squealing," "or "snitching" (to use commonplace prisoner jargon - [not that I have expertise in that area]). The police create different "deals" or incentives to offer to the prisoners in which: 1) the "snitch" will go free for his cooperation providing the other remains silent, and the other will serve the maximum sentence, or 2) if both rat each other out there will be a medium sentence for both. However, if neither confesses they will both serve minimal time on a reduced charge. These offers are presented to each prisoner identically and separately. The result almost invariably entails betrayal because decisions are typically based on self-interest. <u>Even though the prisoners have more to gain from cooperation.</u> The game demonstrates that betrayal trumps collaboration and that self-interest dominates. And so it is in the Money Game and the game of life.

Yes, your competition/opponent will almost invariably operate from self-interest. The naïve, or good-hearted may not fully appreciate this fact, and it can impede their progress in the Money Game.

Emotions are also a large factor in our financial decisions. And, as we learned earlier in this book you will need to expend effort in controlling your emotions and increasing your reliance on objectivity, rational thought processes and thorough analysis. Games are typically won as a consequence of knowledge, thorough preparation, skill, and good decision-making. You could of course, rely on luck, but fate is fickle and you would be foolhardy to count on good fortune to save you.

Game theorists have developed relatively uncomplicated games to test their theories, and have limited options for ease of experimentation and to reduce the impact of extraneous factors. The real world is not that straightforward.

As you can appreciate, game theory and predicting behavior in a logical, reasoned fashion is not so simple. Too many variables enter the picture. In fact instead of a few simple choices you may be confronted with scores of financial options in the course of a single day or week. So you must know yourself well, what you are willing to sacrifice and risk to win the game, how much knowledge, preparation, training and effort you're prepared to commit, etc.

Money Management

If you read a book on gambling you will find a chapter on Money Management. This is an important topic because winners must learn to take some of their winnings "off the table" instead of letting it "ride." Every avid gambler knows this. And, even if you're not a gambler there's a significant element of chance in your life and personal finances. So be prepared.

Along with many other financial experts I advocate setting aside a minimum of 10% of your income. Think of it as "paying yourself *first*."

Some of you will have access to a company-sponsored *401K* plan, or you may want to create an *IRA*, or a *SEP* (Self-Employed investment Plan), or have a brokerage account, or any array of tax-sheltered, deferred, or preferred plans or investments. Even if there is no tax advantage you still need to save and invest.

The most important consideration is to turn that "switch" in your head so that you are in a saving mode rather than a 100% spending and consumption mode. Temptations abound and the game has almost limitless options, alternatives and decisions.

Effective money management is perhaps your most important weapon in the arsenal of effective techniques to keep you competitive and successful in the Money Game. We all know people who have squandered their advantage by ineffectiveness or downright incompetence in handling their finances.

Choices

Your life is all about choices, you're always making them whether you realize it or not. Try to focus on making good decisions. It's a form of "mental accounting." We do our own little analysis. Generally, an individual will opt for stability rather than change. Even if it's not in her/his best interests. We discussed game theory earlier and found that people make decisions that they perceive to be in their best interest, but they don't always make good ones because their analysis may be incomplete or inaccurate. Combine this with the bias toward status-quo and you have a model that conspires to frequently result in poor decisions.

The remedy is to perform a thorough analysis (including cost/benefit), recognize the biases, and make a reasoned decision, perhaps testing it with trusted advisors. Choices are omni-present in the Money Game.

Branding

Recently the concept of "branding" has gained greater import and favor. Businesses brand their companies and their products and have for centuries. Would you rather buy a pair of *Levi's* jeans or a "no-name" brand? A *Coke* or a generic soda?

Now "personal branding" is emerging as viable option and professional differentiator. Perhaps it's always been that way but we didn't appreciate it or label it. Instead of *Ford*, *McDonald's*, a *Kraft* food, a *Kleenex* tissue or an *Apple iPad*, it's the *Ben Carlsen* brand or *your* brand. The *You* brand and the *Me* brand; like we're all commodities. In the final analysis a brand is a reputation and an identity. Your brand represents you to others. If you have a personal brand which conjures "creative," "reliable," "trustworthy," "superior," "high quality," etc., the force is with you.

In the Money Game your brand is important. It will open doors and lead to opportunities, *if it's a good one*. Your brand will typically be linked to your profession so you will be known as a "top attorney," the "best cardiologist," owner of the "finest Mexican restaurant in town," or an "excellent teacher."

Self-Confidence

Building your brand will require a healthy measure of self-confidence. Psychologist Albert Bandura's *Self-Efficacy Theory* provides some insight into this area. Bandura's studies support the premise that greater confidence in your ability to perform will result in measurably better performance. Your sense of self-efficacy can help you succeed.

We're all told to "believe in ourselves" but life experience frequently has a way of knocking us down.

The idea that confidence in oneself's ability will increase the likelihood of good results is a powerful one when it comes to the Money Game. Low perceptions of self-efficacy, self-confidence, ability, self-esteem, etc., may cause you to doubt your performance and skills. It will lead you to believe that tasks are harder than they actually are. This self-doubt can easily translate into lack of trying, pro-crastination, avoidance of challenge and will adversely influence the way you approach life's tasks, challenges and goals.

Some ways to rectify the situation include: positive self-talk, surrounding yourself with supportive individuals, ac-curately assessing your performance, recalling your past successes, realistically assessing challenges (and your prob-ability of success), and taking on new challenges.

Of course some people can overcome self-doubt by using their perceived inadequacies, poor life circumstances or past failures as motivators to excel. Essentially turning negatives into positives. Just recognize that perceptions may be stronger than reality and it's your job to think well of yourself and your potential.

Modeling

Living near South Beach I see plenty of models. The beau-tiful people being photographed at the beach when I take my morning exercise, or lounging around Ocean Drive or Lincoln Road. They represent the peak of physical perfec-tion and they're objects of admiration and envy.

The type of models I'd like you to emulate are those who are succeeding at the Money Game. Whether it's Richard Branson or Oprah Winfrey, Bill Gates, Ted Turner, the late Steve Jobs, Warren Buffet, Carlos Slim, Mayor Bloomberg, etc. You may want to read a biography of one or more of these individuals or you may have someone more up-close-and-personal in mind. There are plenty to choose from. Your successful uncle, your mother or father, your friends or business associates.

Social Learning Theory suggests validity to the folklore that claims "children learn what they see," and "monkey see, monkey do." This is why it's so important that you pick positive role models. The slacker or gangster won't help you improve your life, except as an example of what not to do. And the fashion model won't help either, except perhaps with your style and appearance.

Modeling means you pick someone and study and emulate them. They become a role model of sorts and you "pose" like them, imitate their attitudes and behaviors; learn from their successes and failures. The formula is straightforward: 1) Observe, 2) Imitate, 3) Experience Consequence (reinforcement). So choose wisely who you wish to follow and the behaviors you want to model. If you don't consciously make a choice you will do so inadvertently. The results, positive or negative, will occur either way.

Survival Strategies

In order to succeed a business must offer a product or service which is in demand, people will pay for, and is profitable. You're in a similar situation.

If you work for someone else you will be providing services to them which they will compensate you for in accordance with your perceived value and competitive circumstances. You will contribute to the business and you will be rewarded. As long as that business model works, you're o.k. However, if a business reversal takes place there will be cutbacks. We've all seen plenty of those so be prepared.

If your personal finances reverse you will also be compelled to take action. Occasionally Draconian action. What's the most common business response to a downturn? LAYOFFS.

Staffing reductions are the mainstay of business response to a profitability crisis. Now here's where the analogy diverges. It's more difficult for an individual to accomplish savings by this methodology. What are you going to do, fire yourself? The business would end, because you're the final staff member. You can't fire your spouse -- although you could divorce them. And if you do there's the matter of severance pay (division of property and alimony). If you have children it's even more challenging. It's difficult to "send them packing" unless they're over eighteen, and even then it may be an ethical and emotional dilemma. Cutbacks are never easy although staffing reduction decisions are somewhat mitigated when there's more staff to choose from.

Unlike most businesses (unless you have a large family owned enterprise) your primary source of expense reduction will not come from personnel. You'll have to look elsewhere. Good candidates are the biggest expenses, typically housing, transportation and "expense accounts."

By expense accounts I mean meals away from home (eating out) and other discretionary spending like entertainment, clothing, snacks, hobbies, etc. For many of us the first place to look is consumer debt – especially credit cards. Despite the recent economic downturn, and in some ways because of it, household debt remains high.

So we've determined that you're left with limited options: either reduce expenses or increase income, or both. You need to decide how you're going to proceed. Have a family meeting, if you have a family. Go over your budget. Become familiar with every amount and category of income and expense. Are there ways to increase income through career change, opening or expanding a business, furthering your education, making more strategic investments, converting non-performing assets to income-producing ones? Become serious about analyzing the expense side of the ledger.

Prioritize. What is of most value to you, personally? Cut out or reduce items lower on your priority list. I can't help you decide what's important to you. And I won't. But if successfully competing in the Money Game is important to you I'm confident you'll make the right decisions.

Risk/Reward

One of the key elements of the game is the Risk/Reward equation. This simple formula specifies that, as a rule, your rewards can be greater if you take greater risks. Conversely, less risk will in all probability entail less reward. The problem is that extreme risk can be equated with gambling. And we know that over the long-run gamblers typically lose.

The key is in self-knowledge – knowing your tolerance for risk, and balancing risk against potential for reward so as to maximize your potential for gain while at the same time limiting your maximum loss.

Life involves risk and you must take chances to move forward, choosing safety, or the status-quo is usually an unfulfilling option and a bad success strategy. However, take prudent not reckless risks.

This will require uncompromising fundamental analysis of the risk/reward proposition, assignment of some probability of success, and a serious evaluation of the extent of your ability and willingness to suffer a loss.

Expert Advice

There are experts either at the game and/or in assisting players in developing their Money Game skills. Generally these experts have specialized backgrounds, knowledge and skills in specific areas. For example, there are real estate experts, and those in this field may be further specialized in investment properties, residential, multi-family, commercial, business or industrial properties, financing, foreclosures/ short sales, leasing, rentals, swaps, etc.

There are Financial Planners, Money Managers, CPA's, Investment Bankers, Tax Experts, Stock Brokers, etc., etc. Smart players frequently engage services of some or several of these experts to improve their odds and performance. Of course the financial landscape is peppered with peril and some of these experts are not what they seem. In fact, they may be more interested in winning the game themselves at your expense. There are also downright cheats, inexperienced, inept, or misguided "experts."

It is important that players "vet" their experts before engaging their services and closely monitor and validate the advice provided. Do some basic research, fact and reputation checks. Look for credentials; ask friends for recommendations. In the end the decision is up to you.

Work with people who are true experts, have a good track record, that you trust and are comfortable with. A basic precept is that "nobody cares as much about your money as much as you do!"

Slow and Steady

One strategy that seems to work is the slow and steady approach. As boring as that may sound it works for many players. Avoiding mistakes will help you continue progressing in the game without all the drama that can be encountered from major setbacks. A book that I like citing confirms that strategy. *The Millionaire Next Door* surveyed and interviewed real-live millionaires and discovered that far from being flamboyant free-spending risk-takers, most actually took a rather conservative approach to building their fortunes. If this suits your personality you may want to include it in your game plan.

You Need a Plan

So far we've talked about the concept of personal finance as a game within the larger context of a broad institutionalized economic and money game sponsored, endorsed and perpetuated by society, government, business, etc. and with everyone as a participant. We acknowledge that it's competitive, understand that there's a rudimentary safety net for players who fail, appreciate the fact that there are rules.

There are also penalties for breaking the rules, acceptable tolerances of player behavior, experts in the rules and at aspects of the game. We also know that there are ethical and moral considerations, strategies, risk and reward parameters, etc. You need a personal plan that takes all of these factors into account.

Your plan should include a personal assessment of the extent of your desire to participate and win, an evaluation of your skills, identification of strengths and weaknesses, a selection of arenas in which to play (e.g. investments, professions, commercial and industrial fields, etc.).

Your plan should incorporate a methodology for assessing your performance (and a discussion of score-keeping follows).

Keeping Score

You must keep score. To be effective this will require a Net Worth Statement. Monthly bank statements or quarterly investment account reports are not enough.

Your NWS (Net Worth Statement) will include the cash value of *all* your Assets and list *every* Liability (debt). Serious players will update their NWS monthly, or at least quarterly. You should do the same. You also need to set goals and targets for yourself, realistic and "stretch" goals are fine so that you can compare your actual performance against your pre-established benchmarks.

Keeping score will help motivate you, hold your interest, intensify your competitiveness, and arm you with facts and figures on which to base your decisions, revise your goals and strategies, and achieve your financial objectives.

A friend of mine, after reading this book developed his own methodology to keep score. He devised a system wherein he assigned himself points for behaviors which he felt were advancing his personal Money Game and subtracted points when his actions weren't contributing to his advancement. He used a "board" analogy with forward movement representing a winning game strategy. He maintains that a game well played will result in financial gain. I agree.

You may decide to create your own score-keeping method, or opt to keep track of your progress by monitoring your monthly statements from financial institutions and your NWS. (We'll discuss this more in Chapter six.)

Timing

Timing may not be everything but it's awfully important. If you bought a house in 2006 you probably paid top dollar. Today few homeowners could get what they paid for a home purchased during the go-go years of the late 1990's and early 2000's. Similarly, if you invested large sums in the stock market in the summer of 2008 you also took a hit a few months later and probably haven't broke even yet. And if you're now entering the employment market you'll find fewer jobs often at lower pay and less benefits.

The importance of timing should not be underestimated, but what can you do about it? Not much, in the sense that you can't change it, but you can change your strategies.

Following the housing crash there were bargain properties to be found at a fraction of their earlier price and after the stock market crash there were bargains in equities. The message – don't follow the crowd.

However you can benefit from joining the crowd in the early stages of a boom or rally, then taking some of your profits to be set aside for future opportunities. And you can benefit from the opportunities in the aftermath of crowd mania.

Just like there's an opportune moment to make that winning pass, or strategic play, there will be many Money Game opportunities over the length of the contest. Be on the lookout for them and be prepared to take advantage.

Your Strategic Advantage

Your primary advantage will come from your attitude, motivation and skills. Your perspectives will count! If you view the Money Game as a tedious, unnecessary or uninteresting activity you will probably fail. If you don't take the time and effort to improve yourself and understand the game you'll have a reduced competitive advantage. And if you have the misfortune of playing in a rigged or low stakes game you'll also likely have problems.

So gain every advantage you can. Study the game landscape and learn from better players or experts in the game. If you need to change your player identity, strategy or in what arena you play, do it.

It is possible to train yourself to become a better player and/or to obtain coaching to enhance your potential. In 1972 Timothy Gallwey wrote a book titled "The Inner Game of Tennis" in which he described the attitudes, insecurities, fears and self-doubts of tennis players as translating into performance issues and setting them up for failure.

This is the "inner game" and since that initial breakthrough insight many books, programs and workshops have followed. And the concept broadened to include other sports (e.g., baseball, golf, etc.) and even "work."

This concept of the "inner opponent" is one that carries common-sense validity and demonstrable performance consequences. Just think "I'll never be able to make that shot" and typically in self-fulfilling prophecy fashion – *you won't*. Good players have less self-doubt and excellent players exude confidence. They've done it before and know they can do it again. Tiger Woods is a prime example of negative emotions, self-doubt, and image-conflicts impacting his game. Do you think for a moment that it was coincidental that his golf game went into the toilet following his personal scandal? It takes a long time to overcome severe psychological and emotional trauma. You need to re-program yourself for success. Easier said, than done you may think. And, of course, you're right!

Reframe the way you look at your personal finances and your life. Look at it all as a game. The game perspective opens up new avenues for creativity and enjoyment and should greatly facilitate your road to success.

Most people view their finances from the "have to" model. "I have to go to school." "I have to prepare so I can get a job." "I have to work so I can make money." "I have to make money so I can enjoy life."

But where's the enjoyment in so many obligations, tasks and responsibilities? Reframing to the game paradigm is liberating. Games are FUN. They're competitive. And we PLAY.

It doesn't mean you won't invest time and effort to learn the game and become proficient at it. But it does engender a more positive mindset.

For most of my life I've worked. And worked hard. Beginning at age 14, and even earlier if I include the odd jobs as a child. My parents taught me that life is tough and requires sacrifice. Sure we had good times but work came first. It's almost heresy to think of making money as being fun. But after leaving home and setting out to make my place in the world I realized that many people were making boatloads of money AND having fun! I vowed to be one of them.

This paradigm shift may prove challenging for you. You may even want to engage some of the specialized coaches (advisors) or even a "life coach." Sometimes that will make the difference.

Teamwork

You will probably need a partner in the Money Game. Spouses or "significant others" can fufill that role. Some of the most successful people I know are team players and their "home team" was legally structured by marriage, and/or solidified by love and commitment.

Whether you're a solitary player or a "partner player" teamwork can be advantageous. Join a team of like-minded individuals who will support, encourage, advise, and keep you on track. Modern society is geared more towards a team mentality than an independent "frontiersman" one.

Sometimes you join the wrong team, or select team members who are selfish players, inept, don't want to practice and/or geared for failure. You can always change teammates or change teams.

Take a lesson from professional sports where team members come and go all the time. You will want to draft competent players that will enhance your game and your prospects for winning. Don't be afraid to cut team members who aren't pulling their weight. But before cutting a teammate loose always try to give due consideration, the benefit of the doubt, and opportunity for improvement. In other words, make deliberate, reasoned and responsible personnel decisions.

Joy of the Game

Enjoy the Money Game. Share the joy of the game with your loved ones, your colleagues, fellow players and friends. You'll probably notice more enthusiasm and cooperation as well as better performance. Just remember to constrain your mania when the occasion requires. Life is still serious and on some occasions conspicuous lightheartedness is inappropriate.

I can think of few things that are more fun than legitimately making money (although there are several that come to mind). And, certainly spending money can be a lot of fun too, but you have to have it first.

"It is curious that physical courage
should be so common in the world,
and moral courage so rare."

Mark Twain

CHAPTER FIVE

Ethics

You could cheat. And you might end up winning. But is it worth it? Most of us have principles rooted in parental up-bringing, education, societal values and/or religious beliefs. We may have also developed a sense of fairness, standards for conduct, ethical principles, or the like from our philo-sophical or psychological inquiry and evaluation. Yes, we're human, and we realize that to function effectively in a culture or society there must be some behavioral stand-ards or disintegration into self-centered chaos is inevitable.

However, the game is so important, the potential rewards so great, the incentives so powerful, the temptations to cheat so pervasive, that many players have succumbed to unethi-cal behavior. We're disgusted when we read about stockbroker and investment adviser Bernie Madoff fleecing his clients and friends. We're appalled when we discover that former New Jersey Governor Jon Corzine as CEO of *MF Global* has apparently engaged in illegal and unethical practices and over a billion dollars of client funds went missing. We watch the biggest financial institutions "re-package" mortgages to artificially inflate their value and as a consequence spawn a U.S. housing collapse. We routine-ly witness overcharging, false advertising, exploitation, stock manipulation, insider trading, unwarranted favorable treatment, scams, and so forth.

We see our government engage in Ponzi-like schemes with Social Security, bailouts, incessant borrowing and uncon-trolled spending. Yes, corruption, fraud, misrepresentation, and cheating are all around us.

When you struggle to pay your income taxes and you learn that *General Electric* paid none; zero, "zip" on over fourteen billion dollars in income on their 2011 return you may feel a twinge of outrage. (Of course if you filed a 57,000 page return and had hundreds of tax experts and CPA's working for you, your bracket might be lower too.)

Remember, it's a game. Sometimes the rules are created to reward the powerful, influential or well-connected. Often the rules favor unfair play. Business-like thinking requires that you take advantage of every rule that will benefit you. Playing by the rules can be a strategy in and of itself. If there's a tax loophole that applies – use it. Deductions, rebates, discounts, exemptions are there for a reason. Use them.

You must reconcile your ethics and morals within the context of the game. Let's explore some examples. Most of my life I have been fortunate to make a living in organizations, professions and businesses in which I took pride. I did, however, become employed by a company with questionable ethics, at least by my standards. This made for some uncomfortable decisions and compromises and I was relieved to sever my ties. You may have experienced similar situations.

Perhaps you can't fulfill your obligations and pay your bills. Earlier in this book I mentioned the concept of running your personal finances like a business. So you may have to do what businesses do so often. You might have to restructure, reorganize, default on your debt, declare bankruptcy, modify your mortgage, negotiate better terms on your obligations, etc. There is no shame in this.

These are business strategies to master the game and you would be a fool not to take advantage of them if your circumstances should require these options.

You may be thinking "I could never do that!" Well, there's a difference between playing the game by the rules and cheating. And some people are unwilling to invest the required time and effort to win honestly so they take shortcuts. You should not let false pride, ignorance or a distorted sense of morality get in your way.

If the choice is between putting food on the table and paying an overdue bill which is the most moral alternative? If it's between continuing to live in your home and being forced into uncertain or questionable living arrangements shouldn't you try to come to a mutually agreeable resolution with your mortgage lender? Is that ethical, moral and fair? Sure it is. But you must judge and decide. Should you take your child to the dentist or pay the credit card payment? The MONEY GAME IS FULL OF CHOICES.

The most important distinction is what is your underlying intent? If you intend to mislead, cheat, defraud, take unfair advantage, or bamboozle someone I think you know the answer. You are not behaving ethically. On the other hand, if you made a mistake, "got in over your head," experienced a health crisis or financial reversal, or are using the rules to benefit your particular situation you should be able to do what you have to without remorse, guilt or sleep disturbance.

"I'm a winner each and every time I go into the ring."

George Foreman

CHAPTER SIX

Managing the Game

Don't be discouraged if your name isn't included in the *Forbes* annual Billionaire edition. Few people achieve those lofty heights. But you should aim for winner status. And there are lots of winners. Millions of them.

You have an advantage if you were lucky enough to be born in a developed country, particularly the U.S. or Europe. But developing nations have lots of opportunities too. Consider yourself fortunate if you're not one of those people in the poorest countries who must live on a couple of dollars or day or less. If you are part of any other society you enjoy a substantial head start. And even if you're born "dirt poor" there are plenty of examples of people overcoming all odds by being lucky, clever or determined.

In this book we explored various strategies for winning a game, whether it's a philosophical or mind game, a *Monopoly* board game, a chess game, video game, a sporting contest, a war game (or a real war). The result of this exploration has yielded some nuggets of wisdom and should sharpen your skills. Let's recap the major ones:

Protect your assets, control the "board," preparation and strategy are paramount, know yourself, know your opponent, it's a long contest and early moves are important, reasoned/rational analysis is best, control your emotions, learn from experience, avoid losses, build on success, recognize the role of luck. Study and practice the game to become more expert. Prime and motivate yourself, and perhaps join a team.

Also get advice from those more experienced than you, model successful behaviors, make reasoned decisions, and practice deception when it's required for survival.
And, of course, have fun!

Some Practical Advice

Now let's simplify and focus the money part of the process even further with a practical four-step formula:

1.   Make Money
2.   Spend less than you make
3.   Save and invest
4.   Be consistent and persistent in applying steps 1 through 3

Or, to apply the advice in *The Millionaire Next Door* become a "prodigious accumulator of wealth." According to the authors of that book your net worth should equal at least: One-tenth of your age times your annual income. Let's see: If you're forty and make forty thousand dollars annually, then it's 4x40=$160,000. That's for an average wealth accumulator, not the prodigious one. So if you are goal-setting you may want to consider that advice. Of course the book was written years ago, and in this economy you may think that formula is way off base. The point is to begin moving towards prosperity and establish some goals.

Warren Buffet is one of my favorite money masters and his advice might be the simplest and most important of all. It is summarized in two rules:

Rule no.1   Never Lose Money
Rule no.2   Never forget Rule No. 1

Just because you know the principles, the rules, and the strategies doesn't mean you'll win because it's a "mind game" too. Your attitude, motivation, outlook, style, commitment and resilience will play a huge role. You will play a series of games within the Money Game. Some will be "friendly competition," while others will be cutthroat. It's essential to know the game and the competition so you can capitalize on your strengths and conceal your vulnerabilities. Games are not won in one move, but instead, by a series of well-executed plays.

Luck will have its role but desire, strategy, persistence, skill and motivation will play a larger part. You'll want to "play by the rules," so you don't get penalized or removed from the game. But you also need to be aggressive. Competition is difficult and winning is not for the faint-hearted.

You need to plan your moves, every step forward will get you closer to a win, but don't expect a smooth continuous forward advancement. At times you'll need to step-back, perhaps take a breather, call time-out and re-group. Your body and mind cannot endure an unending series of battles.

Training Camp will be a rejuvenator. We've all been to Conferences and Retreats where we gain an infusion of optimism, learn some new skills, reinforce our worthiness, and gain new perspectives. Take time out for these respites and you'll find yourself eager to get back in the game and playing with renewed enthusiasm and vigor.

A little R&R is necessary and beneficial. Don't think you're slacking off by taking a break. Simply being good to yourself by acknowledging your needs and treating yourself like someone special (you are!) contributes to your winning attitude.

A Step-by-Step Approach

The Money Game does not lend itself to a cookbook recipe: Add 2 teaspoons of luck, an ounce of opportunity, stir in some effort, two cups of work, etc. And everyone's cake won't look the same. But for those seeking some guidelines, here's what they might look like:

Step 1 - Recognize that it's a GAME
Step 2 – Understand that you MUST PLAY
Step 3 – PLAY
Step 4 – LEARN all you can about the game (ongoing process)
Step 5 – Learn from your SUCCESS
Step 6 – Learn from your MISTAKES
Step 7 – Keep PLAYING
Step 8 – Get COACHING
Step 9 – Revise and improve your STRATEGIES
Step 10 –Continually improve your COMPETITIVENESS
Step 11 –Stay MOTIVATED
Step 12 - Know the SCORE
Step 13 –TRY HARDER
Step 14 - ENJOY the game
Step 15 - Play to WIN
Step 16 - Set higher GOALS
Step 17 - Keep LEARNING about the game; watch for rule changes, player changes, PRIZE changes, etc.
Step 18 – STAY AHEAD of the competition
Step 19 – Embrace new TOOLS & TECHNIQUES to gain advantage
Step 20 – Set aside a portion of your WINNINGS
Step 21 – ENJOY your victories
Step 22 – ENJOY YOUR WINNINGS
Step 23 – If you get BEAT or lose a round, accept it with PRIDE & GRACE

Step 24 – GET BACK in the game

Step 25 – For more fun and support make it a TEAM sport

Step 26 – CHANGE the game or the way you play to make it more satisfying

Step 27 – Play HARDER & SMARTER

Step 28 – Encourage NEW PLAYERS

Step 29 – Take a GAME BREAK once in a while

Step 30 – Keep the game in PERSPECTIVE

Step 31 – If you lose, make it a TEMPORARY condition

Step 32 – If you win SHARE your good fortune!

Step 33 – Keep getting coached and COACH others

Step 34 – Earn your REPUTATION as good player and a fair one

Step 35 – Use your reputation to gain LEVERAGE

Step 36 – BEHAVE like a Champion

Step 37 – Strive for DOMINANCE of the game

Step 38 - NEVER GIVE UP!

Step 39 – Achieve MASTERY and WIN the game

Step 40 – Exit the game as successful player with PEACE & DIGNITY

Your life, and your Money Game will not unfold in the neat orderly sequence just described. The steps in the book are merely illustrative, but give you an idea about the complexity of the game and what it takes to master it.

"Those who win become emperors,
those who lose become bandits."

Old Chinese saying

CHAPTER SEVEN

More Money Game Winner Tips

In addition to the strategies and techniques I've discussed and summarized throughout the book here's a final checklist of additional and important game-winning tips for you. You will notice that most of these have to do with things like attitude, commitment, and passion, as I believe these qualities and factors are most important. We've all witnessed players with less "natural ability" prevail over players with those attributes.

There is a brief video used by motivational speakers, educators, training programs and coaches that pretty much summarizes it. The video depicts famous statesmen, celebrities, and other exceptional well-known successful people who have overcome adversity. The title: "If you think you *can*, or if you think you *can't*…Either way, you're right!"

Here's the list for those players that think they can.

1 **STUDY THE GAME**
2 **BE PREPARED TO PLAY (get in condition)**
3 **KNOW YOURSELF**
4 **UNDERSTAND YOUR COMPETITION**
5 **HAVE A GAME PLAN**
6 **SHOW UP FOR THE GAME**
7 **LISTEN TO YOUR COACH(ES)**
8 **GET YOUR "GAME FACE" & GAME ATTITUDE ON**
9 **PLAY YOUR BEST**

10 **TRUST, SUPPORT AND ENCOURAGE YOUR TEAMATES**

11 **DON'T GET DISCOURAGED BY LOSSES OR SETBACKS – Get Back in the Game**

12 **ENJOY YOUR WINS & LEARN FROM YOUR LOSSES**

13 **LEARN TO "LOVE THE GAME"**

14 **PLAY & PLAY AGAIN (realize that you're a life-time player)**

15 **COMMIT TO & DEVELOP EXCELLENCE**

CHAPTER EIGHT

Winning the Game

As we've learned, you decide if you're a winner or loser. Theoretically, we could all declare ourselves winners. But it isn't quite that simple because of the pervasive element of *relativity*. Are you winning more now than you did before? Or as the politicians are fond of saying "Are you better off now than four years ago"?

Similar to so much of life, history and experience, it's all relative! How are you doing in *comparison* to your most important reference groups and benchmark individuals? How are you performing relative to your peers, your family, your friends; local and national census data? More importantly how are you doing with regard to your self-set goals?

Allen Parducci's (UCLA) *Happiness Theory* has as a core premise: Performance and satisfaction are viewed contextually, not independently. We're as happy as we view our performance in comparison to our expectations. And the gap between our perceived reality of our current condition, and our estimation of what we want for ourselves is the source of our dissatisfaction. Logically then, one way to increase our happiness is to reduce or limit our goals and expectations. Don't be tempted by this simple contrivance. Set high, but attainable standards for yourself.

Yes you could be frustrated with your progress along the way, but in the end you will experience greater success and accomplishment. Of course, temper your aspirations with reality.

If your current condition is poverty and homelessness, and you lack skills and education, perhaps your immediate goals should be to eat, get a place to live, and improve your employability rather than making a million dollars. Although I'm not denying that you could make a million (like Will Smith's engaging portrayal of a real life success story in *Pursuit of Happyness*).

There are other factors to consider in your quest for victory in the Money Game. What about RISK? We briefly explored that concept earlier, but it's not the boogeyman you may believe. Remember, there's a *safety net*. We mentioned poverty earlier, and developed countries have programs in place to ensure your survival. If you lose your job you can apply for *unemployment insurance*. If you can't pay your bills you can declare *bankruptcy*. If you're in danger of foreclosure on your home you can try for a *mortgage modification*. If you can't afford food you can apply for *Food Stamps*. And if you get sick you can go to a public hospital or clinic, and use *Medicaid*. If you're old or disabled and can't work there's *Social Security*. And so on. The *Safety Net* may need a few patches but it's there to prevent your complete disintegration when encountering problems or calamities you can't solve on your own. Fortunately, most of us will not experience the most difficult of these situations.

But what happens when you have major or minor setbacks? When you're not playing the Money Game well, or at your peak? The most appropriate responses are: train harder, learn new skills, get coaching, motivate yourself, re-energize your sense of competitiveness, and get back in the game. Real character is revealed not from basking in the glory of winning but in gracefully recovering from defeat.

In this book you have been exposed to so many useful perspectives and winning strategies that you must take personal responsibility if you don't win. Of course I'd love to see you win big! And perhaps you'd even remember me if that happens. (Lol) If you don't win in any significant way I would suspect that lack of interest or effort would be the culprit.

I'm sure you've heard that "practice makes perfect!" No it doesn't, but it should make you better. You can practice the behaviors that prevent you from attaining financial independence or you can practice the life skills that will make you succeed. You can spend all of your income or you can save and invest a bit. You can think of the future or concentrate only on the present. It's all up to you.

Perhaps one more perspective will make the difference. Learn to *Love the Game*! You have to play anyway so you might as well enjoy it! Don't reject it as crass or unwinnable. Have fun! Savor your small successes and relish your big accomplishments. View yourself as a Winner, or a Winner in Training.

"Champions aren't made in gyms. Champions are made from something they have deep inside them— a desire, a dream, a vision."

Muhammad Ali

CONCLUSION

Becoming a Champion at the Money Game takes a lot of time, skill and effort. Playing at a championship level where only the elite compete can be a thrilling experience. Remember, none of these players got there instantly without plenty of setbacks, mistakes and missteps. Also remember that the confidence imbued from a series of successful competitions can be an intoxicating advantage.

Just viewing personal finance as a GAME will help you win. It's empowering when you realize how much control you have and who your opponents are. The perspective of your financial success and economic life as a game may get your competitive spirit going and your creative juices flowing.

You may already be a competent *Ping-Pong* player, or excellent at *Scrabble*. You might be six handicap *golfer*, or amazing at *Jeopardy*. You could even be a successful businessman, a million-dollar investor or a pro or semi-pro athlete in a major sport. If so, you know what it takes to succeed. And you have what it takes. But whether you're competitive by nature, or not; a champion or mediocre player, or even if the only game you're interested in is *making a living* you can do better. The attitudes, skills, motivation, talent, and discipline that made you successful in one endeavor are transferrable to another, and new attitudes and goals can be developed.

Whether you make your living in a sport, an office, or a factory you're playing the Money Game. And now is the time to take it to the next level. And ultimately play in the Championships.

Wake up in the morning with a "Game On!" mindset. You're not going to that job for work or drudgery, you're going to spend your day participating in an exciting contest with considerable financial and psychological rewards. Go into meetings and negotiations with a competitive attitude – recognizing that "win-win" can be a desirable outcome. Do your best in all situations to keep building your brand, advancing your game and adding to your score.

Each successful move is a step forward in the game and ranks you higher in the standings. A setback is only that. Every move will not be perfect or successful. Successful execution of a *series* of moves should be your objective. Because although one move may decide the game in a close competition, generally it is a combination of moves that makes the difference between winning and losing. And the margin of loss IS important. Just like "Horseshoes" where getting "close" counts, in the Money Game, *relativity* means something. Because the game is so long you'll have plenty of chances to win and little successful advances can be a big factor in the outcome.

Game strategies are applicable to all types of life events. For example, figure how to use the rules to your advantage when completing your *IRS* forms, or developing business strategies, or planning your estate.

Cultivate allies, coaches, team players, cheerleaders and supporters in your quest for victory. Maintain a superior and recognizable *brand* that engenders respect, admiration and cooperation -- and makes people want to do business with you. View the events and challenges in your life from a "game" viewpoint.

Your greatest obstacle to winning is yourself and your mindset. And, as in most games, the outcome is determined at least as much by attitude as skill.

We're accustomed to competing. We play sports as children and adults; we are sports spectators as well. We get grades in school and performance appraisals at work. We're competitive by nature and experience and WE LIKE TO WIN.

Many of us, however, fall into a pattern of sufficing. Of making enough money to get by, accumulating enough to live comfortably, and not giving sufficient thought or effort to WINNING the Money Game.

In the final analysis, the game is just that—a game; a competitive endeavor of questionable merit. But you have to play. We live in an economic world within a capitalistic society. The nature of our environment is competitive with limited resources. The necessity to figure out how to capture sufficient resources to sustain yourself and your family will require substantial effort and typically take up a third (or more) of your life.

Some readers may have competed in the Money Game and won; then lost it all. This is not uncommon, particularly with all of the variables involved and the vagaries of the economic, business, and social environment.

A few of these previously successful players may have decided inadvertently or consciously to not play again or to limit their involvement in the game. My best advice is: "You've done it once, and you can do it again," and, "Once a winner always a winner."

Don't let discouragement or failure define you. And remember, if you're still alive, you're still in the game.

A novel published the better part of a century ago, known variously as "The Glass Beads," or "Magister Ludi," by German author Hermann Hesse may provide some insight. In the book a futuristic society has few pursuits with the primary one being an intellectual game encompassing the arts and sciences, indeed all human knowledge with the objective of "mastering the game" by understanding the relationships and connections between all elements. The best player was "Magister Ludi;" the "Master of the Game." In our current society we seem obsessed with money, economics and consumerism. This is our "game." The Money Game.

You might do well to master it.

RESOURCES/REFERENCES

A Beautiful Mind, (film), from the book by Sylvia Nassar, Universal Pictures, (2001).

Bandura, Albert, "Self-Efficacy in Human Agency," *American Psychologist*, vol. 37. No. 2, February, 1982.

Buffet, Warren, *The Essays of Warren Buffet*, Minneapolis: Cunningham Group, (2008). (2nd ed.)

Davis, Gordon D., *Game Theory: A Non-Technical Introduction*, New York: Dover Pubs., (1997).

Either Way You're Right, (training DVD), ATS Media, www.atsmedia.com

Gallwey, Timothy, with Kleiman, Z., and Carroll, Pete. *The Inner Game of Tennis*, New York: Random House, (1972).

Hesse, Hermann, *The Glass Beads, (Magister Ludi),* New York: Holt Reinhart & Winston, (1969).

Kahneman and Tvoskey, Choices, Values and Frames, *American Psychologist*, vol. 39, No. 4, April, 1984

Kaputa, Catherine, *You Are a Brand*, Boston: Nicholas Beasley Pub., (2010).

Machaevelli, Niccolo, *The Prince*, New York: Soho Press, (2011). (paperback ed.)

Millennials Struggle With Financial Literacy, Malcom, Hadley, USA TODAY/ Money, April 17, 2012

Parducci, Allen, *Happiness, Pleasure, and Judgment: The Contextual Theory and Its Applications,* Mahwah, UK: Lawrence Erlbaum Associates, Pub., (1995).

Pursuit of Happyness, (film), from the book by Chris Gardner & Quincey Troupe, Sony Pictures, (2006).

Smith, Adam, *The Money Game*, London: Vintage Books, (1976). (paperback ed.)

Stanley, Thoms J., and Danko, William, *The Millionaire Next Door: The Surprising Secrets of America's Wealthy*, Atlanta, Longstreet Press, (1996).

Trump, Donald, *The Art of The Deal*, New York: Ballantine Books, (2004).

Tzu, Sun, *Art of War*, New York: Basic Books, (1994). (9th ed.)

About the Author

Dr. BEN A. CARLSEN, MBA is author of several books and hundreds of business articles. In addition to being a writer and blogger, he has experience as a businessman, entrepreneur, executive manager, consultant, and college professor.

"Dr. Ben," as he's known to his students, earned his Bachelor's Degree at the *University of Washington* with a major in Psychology, an MBA at *Pepperdine University*, and a Doctorate, majoring in Organization and Leadership, at the *University of San Francisco*. He has personal and professional interest in business management, productivity, economics and finance. His books include: *"Bites of Business," "Personal Financial Survival: A Rescue Plan," "25 Mistakes That Can Prevent Your Financial Success," and "Confessions of an Overspender."*

He lives in Miami, exercises at the beach each morning, and is a movie buff.

"Welcome to the game, Nicky.
We're here to make life...fun."

-Urban Dictionary

www.ingramcontent.com/pod-product-compliance
Lightning Source LLC
Chambersburg PA
CBHW032015190326
41520CB00007B/484